Frank, the movie

Jon Ronson is an award-winning writer
and documentary maker. He is the author of
four bestsellers, *Them: Adventures with Extremists*,
The Men Who Stare at Goats, *The Psychopath Test*
and *Lost at Sea: The Jon Ronson Mysteries*, and
two collections, *Out of the Ordinary: True Tales
of Everyday Craziness* and *What I Do: More
True Tales of Everyday Craziness*. He lives
in London and New York City.

FRANK

Also by Jon Ronson

Them: Adventures with Extremists

The Men Who Stare at Goats

Out of the Ordinary: True Tales of Everyday Craziness

What I Do: More True Tales of Everyday Craziness

The Psychopath Test: A Journey Through the
Madness Industry

Lost at Sea: The Jon Ronson Mysteries

JON RONSON

FRANK

The True Story that Inspired the Movie

PICADOR

First published 2014 by Picador

First published in hardback by Picador 2014
an imprint of Pan Macmillan, a division of Macmillan Publishers Limited
Pan Macmillan, 20 New Wharf Road, London N1 9RR
Basingstoke and Oxford
Associated companies throughout the world
www.panmacmillan.com

ISBN 978-1-4472-7137-6

1 3 5 7 9 8 6 4 2

A CIP catalogue record for this book is available from the British Library.

Printed by L.E.G.O. SpA Vicenza, Italy

Permissions Acknowledgements
Page i: courtesy of Element Pictures/Runaway Fridge Films. Photographer Jonathan Hession.
Page ii: Barney Poole. Page 3: courtesy of Linda Nylind. Page 47: © Shirlaine Forrest.
Page 69: © Neil Taylor. With thanks to Neil Taylor. Page 70: © Arfon Jones.
With thanks to Arfon Jones. Page 72: Picture courtesy of Element Pictures/
Runaway Fridge Films. Photographer Jonathan Hession.

To Stevie Lee

One day in 2005 I was in the park with my little boy when my phone rang.

'Hello?' I said.

'*HELLO!*' yelled Frank Sidebottom.

'. . . Frank?' I said.

'*OH YES,*' said Frank Sidebottom.

We hadn't spoken in fifteen years.

'It's been so long,' I said.

Between 1987 and 1990 I was the keyboard player in the Frank Sidebottom Oh Blimey Big Band. Frank wore a big fake head with a cartoon face painted on it – two wide bug eyes staring, red lips frozen into a permanent half-smile, very smooth hair. Nobody outside his inner circle knew his true identity. This became the subject of feverish speculation during his zenith years. His voice, slightly muffled under the head, was disguised too – cartoonish and nasal, as if he was a man-child pretending to be a nightclub comic. Our act involved us doing amateurish plinkety-plonk cover versions of pop classics such as 'I Should Be So Lucky' and 'We Are The Champions'. Frank was all a little wrong, like a comedian you'd invent in a dream – funny but not funny, meticulous and detailed but repetitive, innocent but nightmarish in a certain light. We rode relatively high. Then it all went wrong.

And now Frank was on the phone. He was ready to stage a comeback. Maybe I could help by writing an article about my time in the band? I said of course I would. When I got home from the park I tried to remember our lives back then.

•

In 1987 I was twenty and a student at the Poly-technic of Central London. I was living in a squat in a huge decrepit townhouse in Highbury, North London. The students who rented proper rooms

Frank Sidebottom

ended up miles away in places like Turnham Green, while the squatters lived for free in salubrious places like Islington and Bloomsbury. It was an otherworldly life. You could find yourself squatting in some abandoned mansion with ballrooms and chandeliers. One group lived for a while in the Libyan Embassy in St James's Square. A staff member had shot out of the window at an anti-Gaddafi protest and a policewoman had been killed. The Embassy staff fled and the squatters moved in.

Most of the squatters were sweet-natured, but sometimes you'd find yourself living with chaotic people who were too frenzied for the mainstream world. In Highbury I'd stand in the kitchen doorway and watch a man called Shep smash all the crockery every time Arsenal lost. He'd grab cereal dishes from the sink and hurl them in a rage across the room, his dreadlocked hair tumbling into his face like he was some kind of disturbed Highland Games competitor or a Dothraki from *Game of Thrones*.

'He is *SO* mentally ill!' I'd think with excitement as I stood in the doorway. Arsenal were destined to lose 25 per cent of their games in the 1987/1988 season, finishing sixth. Shep was a terrifying *Grandstand* football-score service. We were in for a tumultuous time in the communal kitchen. One time Shep noticed me staring at him. 'What?' he yelled at me. I didn't say anything. I felt like a cinema audience watching an adventure movie, emotionally engaged only in the shallowest way. I was just delighted to not be living in Cardiff any more.

In Cardiff, where I had grown up, I'd been bullied every day: blindfolded and stripped and thrown into the playground, etc. It was the sort of childhood a journalist ought to have – forced to the margins, identifying with the put-upon, mistrustful of the powerful and unwelcome by them anyway.

I dreamed about becoming a songwriter. My handicap was that I didn't have any imagination. I could only write songs about things that were happening right in front of me. Like 'Drunk Tramps', a song I wrote about some drunk tramps I saw being ignored by businessmen:

Drunk tramps
Ignored by businessmen
They walk right past you
Don't even see you
But you're the special ones!
With pain but hope in your eyes
Drunk tramps

I did make some money busking on my portable Casio keyboard. There was one song I played fantastically well. It was a twelve-bar blues in C. It was literally the only song I knew how to play. For busking this was fine – nobody stayed around long enough to become aware of my limitations. But one day a man approached me and said he ran a wine bar in Guildford, south-west of London, and did I want to play a set at his club?

'That sounds great,' I said.

I caught the train to Guildford and found the wine bar. I set up my keyboard and played my song. The owner turned to his bar staff and gave them a look to say, 'See?'

After ten minutes I stopped. There was a lot of applause. Then I played my song again but slower.

Then I played it again, but back at the original speed. Someone shouted, 'Play a different song.'

I looked at the crowd. They were evidently puzzled. And irritated. A fake pianist had entered their world and was banging away at the keys, a young man being odd and dysfunctional on the makeshift stage, presumably unaware not just of what was required of a wine-bar pianist but of how to be an adult human in general. Panicked, I hurriedly invented something – an unsatisfactory improvisation around my song. The owner asked me to stop and go home.

.

I went to comedy shows. I'd creep backstage and stand there, looking at the comedians. I saw Paul Merton and John Dowie try and out-funny each other in a gloomy underground dressing room at a club in Edinburgh. Paul Merton made a joke. John Dowie responded with something funnier, then Paul Merton said something funnier still, and so on. Everyone was laughing but it was tense and disturbing, like the Russian roulette scene from *The Deer Hunter*.

Backstage at a different club the comedian Mark Thomas stalked angrily over to me.

'You always just *stand* there,' he said. 'When are you going to *do* something?'

So I decided to try. I put myself forward in the student union election to become the college entertainments officer.

It was to be a year's sabbatical. I'd be in charge of two venues – a basement bar on Bolsover Street in Central London and a big dining hall around the corner on New Cavendish Street. I'd have a budget to put on discos on Fridays and concerts on Saturdays and comedy on Tuesdays. Then after a year I'd return to finish my degree. Nobody stood against me. It was a one-horse race. I was elected.

The entertainment office was on the top floor of the Student Union – a 1960s building in Bolsover Street. I'd sit in the corner, the social secretary elect learning the ropes from his predecessor. I took it all in – how he negotiated fees, dealt with the roadies and the bar staff, even what he said when he answered the phone. He said, 'Ents.'

He warned me that the big music-booking agents tended to see the likes of us as easy prey. If anyone would book their terrible bands it would be us. History would prove this right. I *did* book their terrible bands.

One day I was sitting in the office when the telephone rang. I was alone. My predecessor was off dealing with some issue. I wasn't supposed to answer the phone. But it kept ringing. Finally I picked it up.

'Ents,' I said.

There was a silence. '*What?*' the voice said.

'. . . Ents?' I said.

'Oh,' the man said. 'I thought you said Ants. Jesus! OK. So Frank's playing at your bar tonight and our keyboard player can't make it and so we're going to have to cancel unless you know any keyboard players.'

I cleared my throat. 'I play keyboards,' I said.

'Well you're in!' the man shouted.

I glanced at the receiver. 'But I don't know any of your songs,' I said.

'Wait a minute,' the man said.

I heard muffled voices. He came back to the phone. 'Can you play C, F and G?' he said.

'Yes,' I said.

'Well, you're in!' he said.

The man on the phone said I should meet them at the soundcheck at 5pm. He added that his name was Mike, and Frank's real name was Chris. Then he hung up.

I looked at the receiver.

I arrived at the bar at exactly 5pm. The place was dingy even in daytime – we were deep in a basement – and empty except for a few men fiddling with equipment some distance away across the sticky carpet near the stage.

'Hello?' I called.

The men turned. I scrutinized their faces. In the three hours since the phone call I'd learnt a little about Frank. Frank Sidebottom – how he wore a big fake head on stage and there was much speculation about his real identity. Some thought he might be the alter ego of a celebrity, possibly Midge Ure, the lead singer of the band Ultravox, who had just had a huge hit with the New Romantic song 'Vienna', and was known to be a big Frank Sidebottom fan. Which of these men looking at me might be Frank? And how would I know? If I looked closely would there be some kind of facial indication?

I took a step closer. And then I became aware of another figure kneeling in the shadows, his back to me. He began to turn. I let out a gasp. Two huge eyes were staring intently at me, painted onto a great, imposing fake head, lips slightly parted as if mildly surprised. Why was he wearing the fake head when there was nobody there to see it except for his own band? Did he wear it all the time? Did he *never take it off*?

'Hello, Chris,' I said. 'I'm Jon.'

Silence.

'Hello . . . Chris?' I said again.

He said nothing.

'Hello . . . Frank?' I tried.

'*HELLO!*' he yelled.

Another of the men came bounding over to me. 'You're Jon,' he said. I recognized his voice from the telephone. 'I'm Mike Doherty. Thank you for standing in at such short notice.'

'So,' I said. 'Maybe we could run through the songs? Or . . . ?'

Frank's face stared at me.

'Frank?' Mike said.

'*OH YES?*'

'Can you teach Jon the songs?' he said.

At this Frank raised his hands to his head and began to prise it off, turning slightly away from me, almost as an act of modesty, like he was shyly undressing. I thought I saw a flash of something under there, some contraption attached to his face which he seemed to quickly remove, but I wasn't sure that had happened at all. It was all so fast and discreetly done.

'Hello, Jon,' said the man underneath. He had a nice, ordinary face.

'Hello . . . Chris?' I said.

Chris gave me a sheepish smile, as if to say he was sorry that I had to endure all the weirdness of the past few minutes but it was out of his hands. He took me to a corner and patiently taught me the songs. I picked them up pretty quickly. They were indeed comprised almost entirely of C, F and G. There were one or two other notes, but certainly not the full range. They were mostly cover versions of Queen and Beatles hits.

Before I knew it the public had arrived, and we were onstage. As I played I watched it all – the band assiduously emulating with proper instruments the tinny pre-programmed sounds of a cheap, amateurish children's Casio keyboard, the enraptured audience of about three hundred people, and Frank, the eerie cartoon character front-man, his facial expression immobile, his singing voice a high-pitched nasal twang. I marvelled at the mysterious train of creative thought that had somehow led to this place.

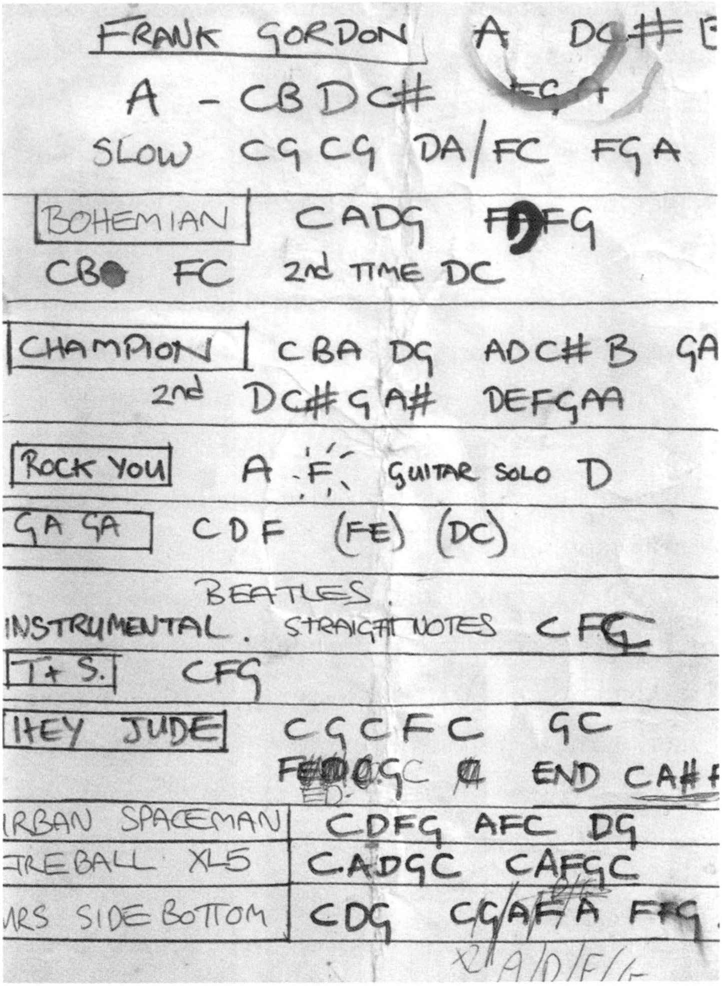

Frank's songsheet

FRANK

Towards the end of the show Frank introduced the band. 'On drums . . . Mike Doherty.' There was a cheer. 'On guitar . . . Rick Sarko. On bass . . . Patrick Gallagher.' He left me until last. 'On keyboards . . . Jon Ronson.' But something unexpected happened. Every other band member had been given a cheer of basically the same volume. But the cheer I received was very noticeably quieter. I was baffled. What had I done wrong? A room full of strangers had for some reason made a unanimous negative determination about me on what seemed the scantest information.

And then, suddenly, I understood. The laissez-faire manner in which I'd been invited to perform in the band that night wasn't the whole story – there had been some furtive professionalism at work. Concerned that I didn't know any of the songs they had at some point decided to turn my volume down to practically zero and position me so far to the edge of the stage that most people in the audience didn't even know there *was* a keyboard player in the band.

That night I trudged home feeling confused.

Frank Sidebottom and Jon Ronson

'Why did they even bother inviting me if they were going to do that?' I thought.

Life went back to normal. A year passed. Then Mike Doherty telephoned me and asked me if I wanted to be in Frank's band full time, and so I immediately told my college I was quitting. Being on the road with a band versus sitting in a lecture theatre learning about structuralism? It was a no-brainer. I moved to Manchester.

And there I was, in the passenger seat of a Transit van flying down the M6 in the middle of the night, squeezed between the door and Frank Sidebottom. Those were my happiest times – when Chris would mysteriously decide to just carry on being Frank. Nothing makes a young man feel more alive and on an adventure than speeding down a motorway at 2 a.m. next to a man wearing a big fake head. I'd furtively watch him as the lights made his cartoon face glow yellow and then black and then yellow again.

●

Jon Ronson and Mike Doherty

I am writing this twenty-six years later. A film I co-wrote, *Frank*, which is fictional but inspired by Frank and our time together, will soon be premiered at the Sundance Film Festival. A few days ago the music journalist Mick Middles sent me 30,000 words from his work-in-progress biography, *Frank Sidebottom: Out of his Head*. His book captures perfectly that 'rarest of journeys' when an onlooker got to see Chris turn into Frank – an 'unsettling' and 'remarkable transformation', he writes. 'The moment the head is placed the change occurs. Not merely a change in attitude or outlook but a journey from one person to the other. I completely believe that Chris was born as two people.' Middles likens Chris to transgender people trapped in the wrong body. Chris was wayward, prone to drink and drugs, but Frank was an ingénue, untouched by 'emotional entanglements, myriad complexities of adulthood, betrayal, hurt, loss, death, fear, tax.'

One passage in Middles' wonderful pages stopped me short. It described his March 2013 visit to Mike Doherty's home. The last I'd heard of Mike he'd emigrated to Bangkok, where he'd made it big as a drummer and a tour manager in the Thai music scene, whatever that meant. But it turned out that he'd had a serious motorcycle crash and was now back in 'Stockport's unfashionable Cheadle Heath', living with 'an amiable cat, Bob.' Forced into retirement, Mike had 'set about, armed with only a felt tip pen, to completely transform every room in his house via a maze of complex designs, mostly intended to celebrate his time with Frank, Manchester music in general plus the odd nod to his beloved Manchester United.' Middles describes the designs as having been 'stenciled with great wit. I like to think, rather than an indication of a man with too much time on his hands, the flat is a true indication of a still-lively artistic mind . . . and talent!'

There in Cheadle Heath, Mike Doherty told Mick Middles why he'd invited me to join the band. Having no idea how I came across to people back then, it was a great compliment: 'It was always difficult to get people to play in that band because there was absolutely no kudos,' Mike told Mick Middles. 'I mean, who the fuck wants to travel to Bradford or somewhere like that just to play plinkety piano?

There is no artistic merit at all and you are hardly going to get any groupies, are you? So it had to be a certain kind of person . . . someone who has absolutely nothing to prove and understood Frank completely.'

I'm glad Mike Doherty saw me that way but it wasn't true. My expectations for life back then were exceedingly low and being in Frank's band provided me with more kudos than I'd imagined possible. Five hundred people in Bradford was a sea of faces stretching to the horizon. We may have had no artistic merit but we had the accoutrements – drums, leads, amps. We were very much sort of like a band.

But Mike was right about one thing. I got Frank completely. His comedy came from the juxtaposition between the parochialism of his ordinary life and the grandiosity of the songs he covered, like 'Born in Timperley' (to the tune of 'Born in the USA'): 'I go shopping in Timperley / They've got loads of shops / That's where I do the shopping for my mum / Five pounds of potatoes and loads of chops.'

Frank was our Pee-wee Herman. He was silly, unpretentious, irresponsible, homemade. He aimed low. That's why people loved him. He was a child in a northern town remaining assiduously immature in the face of adulthood.

Frank may have been a paean to ordinariness but Chris wasn't ordinary. He was nothing like anyone I'd ever known. He wore a big fake head for very long stretches, for a start. And he was secretive about his home life. I knew he was married with children, but he wasn't like any husband and father I'd experienced. My father ran a wholesale warehouse in Cardiff. He imported cutlery. He played bridge on Tuesdays and Thursdays and golf on Saturdays and watched TV the rest of the time. My father wasn't a chaotic man. Chris was chaotic. Sometimes, on the way back from some gig, I'd become aware that we were taking a detour to some house somewhere with some women we somehow met along the way. There would be partying. In the van I'd listen to his stories, trying to understand him. He reminded me of George Bernard Shaw's unreasonable man: 'The reasonable man adapts himself to the world; the unreasonable one persists in trying to adapt the world to himself.

Therefore all progress depends on the unreasonable man.' Chris was the unreasonable man, except the world never did adapt to him and he never made any progress. Like when Frank was asked to support the boy band Bros at Wembley. There were 50,000 people in the crowd. This was a huge stage for Frank – his biggest ever, by about 49,500 people. It was really his chance to break through to the mainstream. But instead he chose to perform a series of terrible Bros cover versions for five minutes and was bottled off. The show's promoter Harvey Goldsmith was glaring at him from the wings. Frank sauntered over to him and said, 'I'm thinking of putting on a gig at the Timperley Labour Club. Do you have any tips?'

•

I never understood why Chris sometimes kept Frank's head on for hours, even when it was only us in the van. But years later I met another man who also chose to remain masked for long periods, and perhaps his explanation applies to Chris. The man is a real-life superhero named Urban Avenger. He journeys out into the San Diego night looking for crimes to thwart. He told me that he loves being masked. 'When I wear this, I don't have to react to you in any way. Nobody knows what I'm thinking or feeling. It's great. I can be in my own little world in here.'

'I know exactly what you mean,' I agreed with Urban Avenger. 'I was once at a Halloween party and I didn't take off my mask all night. It completely eliminated all social anxiety.'

'Sometimes I wish I never had to take the mask off,' said Urban Avenger.

But if that was Chris's reason too I suspect he'd have denied it. He liked to portray himself as carefree – the more chaotic and marginal and accident- and failure-prone his life became, the happier he claimed to be. But I think it was more complicated than that. I'd noticed something about him. During that first afternoon I'd scrutinized everyone's faces in the hope of some kind of visual clue as to which one was Frank – it turned out that I'd been on to something. Under the head Chris would wear a swimmer's nose clip. It was cumbersome, like a mini-orthopaedic brace. Chris would be Frank for such long periods the clip had deformed him slightly, flattened his nose out of shape. When he'd turn his face away to remove the peg after a long stint I'd see him wince in pain. Furthermore, as Chris's former wife Paula told Mick Middles, 'He could be very attentive, romantic even, but he had a tendency to switch off and think only of Frank. When he started staying up all night, obviously it hit me. I think I resented Frank because of that.'

One night, during a long drive home, Chris told me Frank's origin story. He'd invented him three years earlier, in 1984, when Chris was twenty-nine. He'd been playing in unsigned bands since he was fifteen and had, Middles writes, 'steadfastly kept every [record company] rejection letter . . . hundreds, bulging from a Green Flash tennis shoe box stuffed under his bed. By night he would unearth this treasure, marvelling at the sheer scope and hopelessness of his quest.'

The funny thing was, Chris's band The Freshies was gaining quite a following when Chris made the sudden and bewildering (for his friends and loved ones) U-turn into Frank. His first Sidebottom move, he told me, was to record a cover version of 'Material Girl' and send it around the record labels with the covering letter, 'I'm thinking of getting into show business. Do you have any pamphlets?' An intrigued executive at EMI invited him in for a meeting. Chris arrived as Frank.

'Have you been in show business for long?' the A&R man asked him.

'Oh,' said Frank. 'About' – he looked at his watch – 'ten seconds, actually.'

His debut EP, released on EMI, charted at about number 90 before disappearing. EMI dropped him. But by then he'd built up enough of an audience that we could play to 500 people a night in almost any town in the north of England and London (although those numbers dropped significantly everywhere else in Britain/the world). I rented a flat above a wool shop in Gorton, south-east Manchester and, when I wasn't touring with Frank, managed the indie band The Man From Delmonte, who I'm certain would have become very successful had they teamed up with less inept management.

With Frank I crisscrossed the north of England – Leeds and Bury and Sheffield and Liverpool – and down to London, playing the same venues over and over again. The familiarity became comforting: the Adelphi, Hull; Dingwalls, London; Burberries, Birmingham.

Burberries, Birmingham
Popular music venue for 'alternative' acts in the latter half of the 80s, now defunct, having apparently expired sometime in 1990. Was located at 220 Broad Street. Lush, Ride, Blur, Charlatans, Chills, Pixies all played here . . . The club mutated into Tramps, which subsequently closed in 1992. The site was razed in 2003 and became a car park. No other info available.

– www.thirdav.com

We supported Jonathan Richman and the Modern Lovers at the Town and Country Club in London, and Frank – playing solo – supported Gary Glitter at some student union fresher ball. Glitter's roadies were extremely rude, Chris later told me, cornering Frank and issuing a list of do's and don'ts: 'You aren't allowed to use our lights. Stay away from our hydraulic stage.' Under the head, Chris was seething. As soon as Frank went on, he jumped onto the hydraulic floor, which set off smoke bombs and rose dramatically above the heads of the audience. '*Come on! Come on!*' sang Frank. '*Do you want to be in my gang?*' He spotted Gary Glitter's roadies pushing their way through the audience towards him. After his set he jumped off stage and ran down the corridor, pulling off his head and costume as he went – he had his own clothes on underneath – just as the roadies caught up with him.

'Did you see Frank Sidebottom?' they asked him.

'He went that way,' said Chris.

Frank wasn't the only outsider artist on our circuit. There was Edward Barton, a quiet, bearded man who would stand on stage and scream, 'I've got no chicken but I've got five wooden chairs.' He was the

son of a Royal Air Force officer and he maintained
the polite, formal bearing of his upbringing. He kept
his belongings in a tiny satchel. He travelled home
with us one night and we dropped him off in the
early hours in his neighbourhood, Hulme – a deso-
late housing estate near the city centre. Hulme was
an exceedingly failed 1970s experiment in social
housing. The idea had been to make it a kind of
Brutalist Bath – Georgian crescents reimagined in
raw concrete. They called the crescents Charles Barry
Crescent and John Nash Crescent, names that had
taken on a savage poignancy by the late 1980s now
that Hulme was crumbling, infested with cockroaches
laying their eggs amid the asbestos. The heroin addicts
had moved in – including, unexpectedly, Nico from
The Velvet Underground. The walkways in the sky
were police no-go areas. But the most apocalyptic
thing about Hulme was the packs of wild dogs that
roamed the crescents, feeding on God knows what.
You'd hear them howling in the darkness as you'd
run frantically home from a night at the Hulme Aaben
cinema. We opened the van door to let Edward Barton

out. As he climbed down, with his satchel clutched to his chest, the clasp broke and it opened, all his possessions falling onto the floor.

We drove off, but I kept looking at him from the back window. He made no attempt to bend over and pick up his belongings. He just stood there, his head bowed, staring at the scattered debris. It seemed like I was watching a man at exactly the moment he had reached his nadir. I was confused. From where I stood, Edward Barton was living the dream. He was a decade older than me and had managed to become a fixture on the circuit. He was secure. If he wanted to play Burberries, he could play Burberries. The same went for the Witchwood, Ashton-under-Lyme; the Leadmill, Sheffield; the Duchess of York, Leeds; the Citadel, St Helens . . . As I looked at him I felt a sudden flash of alarm. Was this not enough? Should I have more ambition? Should I be aiming higher? But the feeling quickly passed. I was in the Frank Sidebottom Oh Blimey Big Band. These were halcyon days. The Transit van turned the corner.

*

We carried on crisscrossing the north of England. Our hard work and long hours were paying dividends. The audiences of 500 in every town had grown to 750 and sometimes even 1,000. It was consequently baffling for me to become aware of a growing sense of discontent in the van.

Chris had been in the habit of asking his friends and relatives to perform cameos between the songs on his records. They'd take the form of little skits – conversations between Frank Sidebottom and his milkman or grocer or whoever. In this spirit he had asked his brother-in-law's friend Caroline Aherne – a secretary working at the BBC – to voice the part of Frank's neighbour, Mrs Merton. Afterwards, Caroline decided to keep Mrs Merton going. She somehow got her own TV show, *The Mrs Merton Show*. She won a BAFTA and a British Comedy Award for it. Her follow-up series, *The Royle Family*, won about seven BAFTAs. The *Royle Family* Christmas Day specials attracted audiences of 12 million. A poll organized by the British Film Institute voted *The Royle Family* the thirty-first best television show of all time. And meanwhile we were crisscrossing

Manchester and Bury and Leeds and Sheffield and Liverpool in our Transit van.

Chris's disgruntlement wasn't that Caroline had *robbed* him of Mrs Merton. She hadn't. As Mike Doherty told Mick Middles: 'She was really funny . . . a natural. All she took was the name. I have no doubt that, somehow, Caroline Aherne would have made it to the top. It just so happened that she did it with a Frank character's name.'

The band's guitarist Patrick Gallagher added to Middles: 'It wasn't Caroline's fault. Chris was totally out of control. Whereas, say, Caroline Aherne had a single vision and could just pursue that, Chris might have a fantastic idea, spend some time gaining interest and developing it and then, just as the point where it might actually get somewhere, he would spin off onto something completely different. That's OK for a while but it tended to piss people off because they never knew where they stood.'

Chris never accused Caroline of plagiarism, not even in private. The worst I ever heard him say was that maybe she could have given Frank some recognition in interviews. By then she was forever on the front pages of the British tabloids, under headlines like:

A very fragile superstar

When she surveys the lights of London's West End from her new £800,000 penthouse flat off Carnaby Street, Caroline Aherne ought to feel as if she really has reached the top. The daughter of Irish immigrants Bert and Maureen, she grew up on a council estate in Wythenshawe, Manchester, and her first job was answering the phones at the BBC offices in Manchester.

Today, she is acknowledged as an original and immensely talented writer and actress. She is now a wealthy young woman, garlanded with awards and hailed as a comic genius.

She has, of course, had her problems. A broken marriage, a drink problem and a string of failed romances drove her to a suicide bid, intensive therapy, and eventually escape to Australia.

It is a year since she left Britain, saying that she no longer wanted to be famous. 'I've played the fame game long enough and I just want to disappear,' she said.

Alison Boshoff, *Daily Mail*

It was hard not to feel jealous. And it wasn't only her. Suddenly everyone around us was becoming famous. My next-door neighbour Mani had a band. They became The Stone Roses. Our driver Chris Evans left us to try and make it in radio. By 2000 he was earning £35.5 million in a year, making him Britain's highest-paid entertainer (above Lennox Lewis at second and Elton John at third). Edward Barton, who I'd last seen staring at his scattered belongings in Hulme in the middle of the night, wrote the song 'It's A Fine Day'. It was covered by the group Opus III, became a huge hit, and was sampled by Kylie Minogue in her song 'Confide in Me'. And we kept crisscrossing the country, playing to 1,000 people, sometimes 750, sometimes 500. Still, there were happy times. Like when we played in London and on the way to the venue our driver said the funniest thing I'd ever heard anyone say. He pulled the van up on Edgware Road and wound down the window.

'Excuse me?' he said to a passer-by.

'Yes?' the man said.

'Is this London?'

There was a silence.

'Yes,' said the passer-by.

'Well where do you want this wood?' he said.

•

There is always a moment failure begins. A single decision that starts everything lumbering down the wrong path, speeding up, careering wildly, before lurching to a terrible stop in a place where nobody is interested in hearing your songs any more. With Frank I can pinpoint the exact moment failure began.

'Chris wants to have a rehearsal,' Mike told me over the phone one day.

There was a silence. 'Chris wants a *rehearsal*?' I said.

'Yes,' Mike said, after a moment.

'Why would Chris want to *rehearse*?' I said.

'To take things up a level,' Mike said.

'Take things *up* a level?' I said. I paused. '*Where* are we going to rehearse?'

'At Chris's house,' said Mike.

Mike was trying to sound enthusiastic. But I think he was worried too.

Chris's house was in a normal, nice, modern cul-de-sac a long walk from Altrincham station. His children were playing in the street outside. His wife, Paula, answered the door. I can't remember what she said to me but I recall being struck by how smart and funny she was in that dry, dour Manchester way. She told me to go to the spare bedroom. I walked up the stairs, passing the bathroom door. It was open. I glanced in. Staring back at me from the sink was Frank's head.

'In here, Jon,' I heard Chris shout from a room at the end of the corridor.

I opened the door. And stopped. Things were different – ominously so. A new man was standing there. He wore a maroon shirt tucked smartly into neat black jeans. A bass guitar hung around his neck. As I walked in he started playing a tight soul-funk riff with seeming nonchalance, like it was just something his fingers did, but I understood it to be an act of aggression. He was marking his territory. Chris looked impressed by the man's adeptness.

'Don't you manage that shit band The Man From Delmonte?' the man muttered indifferently.

'Who . . . *are* you?' I said.

'I'm Richard,' he said. 'From The Desert Wolves.'

The Desert Wolves were an '80s indie band in the vein of Lloyd Cole and the Commotions who wrote songs with lyrics like 'We could go driving down Mexico way / The wind in your hair / You look lovely this time of year'. I'd like to say that during the twenty-five years that have passed since Richard took an instant dislike to me in Chris's spare bedroom, a dislike that only intensified during the months that followed before the band imploded, and climaxed in him yelling at me during one tense soundcheck that he'd like to break my 'keyboard playing fingers', he went on to have a disappointing life. But he didn't. He became one of the world's most successful tour managers, looking after Woody Allen and The Spice Girls, and he currently manages the Pixies.

Richard was not the only proper musician Chris brought in to make us more professional-sounding.

The Desert Wolves, Richard is top right

A skilful guitarist and a saxophone player turned up in the spare bedroom too. Mike counted us in with his drumsticks. And it began. We sounded like an excellent 1980s wedding band – the kind of band that could do note-perfect versions of 'Eye of the Tiger' and 'Girls Just Want To Have Fun'.

Chris told me to book us the biggest tour we'd ever undertaken. Thirty dates in thirty days. We'd play every venue that had ever had us on. He choreographed it so I would begin the show. I'd walk on stage, alone, into a spotlight, and play a powerful C with my left forefinger. The synth brass tone – the most stirring of all the Casio tones. This lone note could last a minute or more – it would be up to me to judge at what point the audience were at a peak of anticipation – and then I'd play with my right forefinger, G, F, G, A, F, G. 'Born In Timperley' (our version of 'Born in the USA', Timperley being the Manchester suburb where Frank and Chris lived). 'Born In Timperley'. This would be the cue for the rest of the band to join me on stage for our power-rock reimagining of the song.

The day the tour began we hired a people-carrier

instead of a Transit van and we set off to our first venue. The mood en route was noticeably more pumped. The old Oh Blimey Big Band members had a certain frail avant-garde loucheness to them. But this new band: I felt like I was in a college sports team. We soundchecked. The audience arrived. The place was packed. And then I walked out into the spotlight.

And in the space of that first song – that single 'Born in Timperley' – the audience veered from fevered anticipation into puzzlement into hoping we were playing a weird joke on them into realizing with regret that we were not. What had become of our beloved plinkety-plonk sound? We were Mrs Merton being backed by Survivor. I did my best to covertly sabotage the musical direction from within, being as plinkety as I could muster, playing lots of bum notes, but my influence was limited, drowned out in an onslaught of '80s rock. After a few nights the *NME* savaged us in a live review. By the end of the tour we were playing to almost empty houses. Chris returned to Manchester to a court summons. He owed £30,000 back tax. On the day of his court appearance he stood up in the dock. The judge told him it was a very serious matter and had he considered a payment plan?

'Would a pound a week suffice, m'lud?' he asked.

'No it would not!' the judge shouted.

Chris never actually said to me, 'You're fired.' But I began to notice in the listings magazines that he was doing a lot of solo shows – just him and a keyboard. They were in the same venues we used to play, and then in smaller venues, and then eventually there were no shows at all.

I moved back to London.

•

And there I was, two years later, twenty-five and presenting a terrible BBC2 television show nobody remembers called *The Ronson Mission*. After leaving Frank's band I'd become a radio presenter at KFM in Stockport and a columnist for *Time Out* magazine in London. My old college lecturer Frank Hatherley had approached the BBC's Janet Street-Porter on my behalf, suggesting me as a presenter, and they'd given me a chance. Now I was sitting in the corner of the editing suite watching the producer, director and editor work on an interview I had done in Bournemouth with a Conservative town councillor. For most of the interview she'd been perfectly nice. But at times – when irritated by my line of questioning – she'd become screechy and short-tempered. In the editing suite they were carefully stitching together her screechiest moments, whilst meticulously deleting the normalness.

I watched this black magic. 'Is this bad?' I asked from the corner.

The producer gave me a patient look. 'Think of it this way,' he explained. 'One interviewee suffers, but millions are entertained.'

I grinned nervously. He was right. This was OK. She was a Tory councillor. We were in the tradition of the great caricaturists like Hogarth. And history proved us to be pioneers. During the 1990s the approach we adopted with the town councillor became fashionable. Journalists in magazines and newspapers and on radio and TV would take the furthest reaches of their interviewees' personalities – the hysteria, the pomposity, the passive-aggression, the delusions of grandeur – and stitch them together, deleting the ordinariness. We were defining people by their flaws. I did it to Tory grandees, white suprem-acists, anti-Semites, Islamic militants, and then conspiracy theorists, psychics and, eventually, hippies. We didn't think hard about what we were doing. We did it because people liked it. The more we did it the more successful we were. But if we had thought hard we might have realized that we were contributing to what was becoming a conservative, conformist age. 'If you behave like *that*', our stories said, 'people will laugh at you. They aren't normal. *We're* normal! *This* is the average!' We were defining the boundaries of normality by staring at the people outside of it.

One night in the midst of this I stood wearing a tuxedo outside Grosvenor House, a five-star hotel on Park Lane, Central London. Downstairs in the banqueting hall I had just not won a radio award so I'd gone out for air and spotted another non-winner – the radio presenter Adam Buxton. He was leaning against some railings. I stood next to him for a while.

We watched the limousines speed down Park Lane, the winners spilling out of the hotel in their tuxedos.

'You know why we always lose?' Adam suddenly said to me.

I shook my head.

'Don't you see?' he said. 'You and me? We're marginal.'

I looked at him.

'The things we like,' Adam continued, 'they're *marginal*.'

'You're *right*!' I said, my eyes widening. 'We are *marginal*!' I felt a great weight lifting. I'd spent years frantically reaching for the mainstream – but I didn't have to. It was fine. I was marginal. I could still tell those stories but they could do something else – they could de-humiliate, dignify.

And not long after that I was in the park with my little boy when my telephone rang and it was Frank Sidebottom.

'How *are* you?' I said.

'Oh I'm very well actually, Mr Ronson,' Frank said.

'Frank,' I said. 'Will you put Chris on?'

There was a silence.

'Hello, Jon,' said Chris, in a normal voice.

Chris filled me in on the past ten years. Mike was living it up somewhere in Thailand. Chris, now divorced from Paula, was an animator on the children's claymation series *Pingu*, about the adventures of a penguin living at the South Pole. He loved the work but missed Frank and wanted to bring him back from retirement. I held my breath. I knew from watching *The Blues Brothers* what was about to happen. He'd say he was putting the old band back together. I'd say, 'Of *course* I'll play!' But he never did ask. Instead he said he was wondering if I'd write something about my time in the band to help him with the comeback. Maybe for the *Guardian*? He'd just had some new portraits done by the photographer Shirlaine Forrest. He emailed them to me. I opened the attachment. Time hadn't ravaged Frank. He looked exactly the same.

The telephone call happened to coincide with an abnormally opulent moment in my life. George Clooney was turning my book *The Men Who Stare At Goats* into a film. All this was happening thousands of miles away in Puerto Rico. On the day filming started I sat in my room in North London and looked at online paparazzi pictures of George Clooney sunbathing at the Puerto Rico hotel and playing basketball with the crew. I ought to have been delighted but a deep gloom descended instead. 'They must be having *unimaginable fun*,' I thought. 'And here I am in this *tiny room*.'

I telephoned the film's screenwriter, Peter Straughan. 'I'm feeling very out of sorts – almost *depressed* – and I think the only way to get better is to visit the set,' I said. We flew to Puerto Rico.

We arrived late at night at the hotel. The air was hot and wet and we found one of the producers sitting alone by the swimming pool. He said to me, 'The most exciting day of your life is your first day on a Hollywood film set. The most boring day of your life is your second.'

And so it transpired. My psychological itch was scratched within minutes of arriving on set the next morning. It was in a disused chemical factory near a rainforest an hour out of town. It had only recently become disused and there were still signs above sinks

Frank Sidebottom

that read Emergency Eye Wash. It was exciting to be in such a place. George Clooney introduced himself to me, was very nice, talked about Darfur. Then word got around that the *author* was on set and crew members – costume designers and art-department people – clustered around to meet me. But within a few hours the people who had earlier glanced excitedly at me were now looking surprised that the *author* was still on set for some reason. It turned out that they weren't having unimaginable fun. They were working very long hours in a disused chemical factory. They were exhausted. It was good to discover that my life wasn't necessarily that much worse than George Clooney's life. That evening I suggested to Peter that maybe we should spend the next day sitting at the hotel pool instead. Which was where we began talking about Frank. Could the story I'd written for the *Guardian* be adapted into a film?

A few weeks later Frank was playing at a pub near my flat – the Bull and Gate in Kentish Town, North London. I found Chris in a dressing room at the back, Frank's head in a bin-bag at his feet.

'How did you lose so much weight?' I asked.

'I don't know,' he said, looking pleased.

'Are you exercising?' I said.

Chris shook his head and shrugged. It was a mystery.

'Well, whatever you're doing,' I said, 'you look great.'

Later, we walked across Kentish Town Road so Chris could buy some cigarettes – a cheap and obscure brand I'd never heard of. He'd already given us his approval on the film and I told him the latest news. Film Four wanted to fund its development. They had a director in mind too – Lenny Abrahamson. I'd loved his film *Adam & Paul*, a melancholic slapstick comedy about two Laurel and Hardy-ish junkies wandering around Dublin for a day.

I remembered something Stanley Kubrick's old business-affairs manager Rick Senat had told me about the film business. I'd met him when I was making a documentary about Kubrick. 'What you need to know,' he'd said. There was a flicker of rage in his eyes. 'Films. They *never get made*.' I know screenwriters in their forties and fifties who have spent their lives never getting a film made. Los Angeles is full of those people – spectral figures in cafes in West Hollywood, killing the mornings by hiking on Runyon Canyon, long, empty months peppered with meetings with producers who tell you you're the greatest screenwriter of your generation. And then: nothing. The actor Stephen Mangan has said of Hollywood, 'They kill you with encouragement.'

Even so, I had a feeling that this film might get made. What major star wouldn't want to play a man in a big fake head? Plus my story in the *Guardian* had a coming-of-age quality to it, like *Stand By Me* but with a man with a big fake head.

But – and Chris and I shuffled awkwardly around the question – what would the film actually be *about*? Specifically, Chris wondered, would *Chris* be in it? Chris had said from the beginning that we could do what we wanted with the story. But this part seemed to worry him. However the film might depict Chris, any reality would surely damage Frank.

I had similar concerns. Chris always portrayed himself as untroubled. Whilst a total dearth of anxiety was a fantastically enviable character trait in real life, how could we write a film about a man who just didn't care when everything went wrong and in fact found disaster funny? There has to be something for someone to *lose* in a film, doesn't there? And if Chris was secretly more obsessive about Frank than he let on, how would he feel if the film reflected that? When I considered these complications – the potential for hurt feelings, the possibility that we'd have to carefully manipulate certain facts whilst maintaining the illusion of truth – it suddenly seemed too stressful an endeavour to embark upon.

But there was a solution. It was something Peter had said back in Puerto Rico. And now I said it to Chris. What if we fictionalized the whole thing? We could forget the facts of the story but keep the themes. It could be about the world of marginal music – a celebration of people who were just too odd to make it in the mainstream, even if they had wanted to. It could be a fable instead of a biopic.

Anyway: who would want to write a music biopic? There's always the moment that laboriously shoehorns into the plot whatever *thing* the person is noted for. Like in *The Karen Carpenter Story* when Karen reads about herself for the first time in *Billboard*. She's delighted – 'Close To You' has just entered the top ten – but as she scans the article her face drops. She reads aloud: '"His *chubby* sister"?' Then there's *Summer Dreams: The Story of the Beach Boys*, when Dennis Wilson is introduced to Charles Manson at a party: 'I hear you picked up one of my girls hitchhiking in Malibu yesterday,' Manson says. And then, about five seconds later, 'I predict a race war's coming that will be the end of the world as we know it.'

Chris said he liked the idea of us fictionalizing the story and Peter and I began writing the screenplay, with Lenny joining us after a couple of years. I'd write for a month, send it to Peter, he'd write for a month, send it back to me, we'd send it to Lenny, and around again. It was the opposite of journalism. In journalism you write what's unfolding in front of you. Journalism is a game with rules. In journalism what's acceptable is what happened, and what's not acceptable is what didn't happen. But with fiction comes a daunting infinity. I remember staring blankly at Peter the first time he patiently said to me, 'It doesn't *matter* that it didn't happen. We *make it up*.' Fiction seemed all about harnessing infinity. In fiction when you walk into a restaurant and you sit down there's nobody there and the restaurant doesn't exist. The restaurant is a horrific never-ending nothingness. So you make scattershot decisions about what the restaurant might look like, and who you might be sitting with. You ask of your barely invented person: 'Would they do *this* or *this* if, say, *that* happened to them?' And one day you realize your decisions are no longer haphazard, but informed by things you've already written. And that's when fiction and journalism meet. You have a mass of material and you start to whittle it down, like a sculptor chipping away at a slab. You make choices about what to lose – morally, and also because you want to write a page-turner. And at the end, whether it's fiction or non-fiction, you have a story.

But with screenwriting there's a further leap of

the imagination. It's of no consequence whether your film reads well. The most beautifully written dialogue might be clunky and implausible when performed by actors. In fact the more beautifully written it is, the more implausible it's likely to sound. Plus we cinema audiences are unforgiving. If we realize a scene has told us nothing we didn't learn from a previous scene, we are outraged. We feel bored and trapped. 'Films *eat up* ideas,' Peter once told me. You can have the greatest idea of your life. You put it into your screenplay. It lasts half a page: maybe thirty seconds of screen time.

Our Frank was no longer Frank Sidebottom, so who was he? Although he was, and is, an entirely fictional character, it was fun to journey down a rabbit hole of research into the worlds of other great musicians who'd ended up on the margins, each for very different reasons. Some were natural eccentrics, others prone to anxiety or mania, others still victims of peculiar external circumstances. They were people like the Austin, Texas singer-songwriter Daniel Johnston. The early demos he recorded on a pump organ in his brother's garage – 'Hi, How Are You' and 'Yip/Jump Music' – were masterpieces. This was the summer of 1983. He was so enthusiastic and tireless that when someone wanted to hear his music he'd sometimes – instead of just copying the demo – run home to re-record every song from scratch on a new cassette.

But his enthusiasm got more frenzied and his songs and career turned into a battle between his talent and his manic depression. When he sang, 'I had lost my mind / You see I had this tiny crack in my head that slowly split open / And my brains oozed out / Lying in the sidewalk / And I didn't even know it,' he meant it. A film about him, Jeff Feuerzeig's *The Devil and Daniel Johnston*, is the best documentary about mental illness I have ever seen. It captures how he grew increasingly delusional during the late 1980s, repeating phrases such as 'Kick Satan out' over and over, talking too fast, like he was a passenger in his own thought process.

An uneasy relationship formed between him and his audiences. The crowd would look at each other for clues to how they should respond, what they should think, whether they should like him or not. The moment in the documentary that stayed with me most powerfully was an interview with Daniel's friend Louis Black, the editor of the alternative magazine the *Austin Chronicle*. He once found Daniel standing knee-deep in a river on the University of Austin campus, preaching loudly into the night about Satan.

'We spend our lives with the notion of the crazy artist,' Louis Black said, 'Van Gogh cutting off his ear, and we really loved the crazy people because they were our people. They didn't have any commercial sense. And yet here was a real sick person. And we were, "What are we going to do?" So we did the most pedestrian thing possible. We committed him. I've always had contempt for those people who didn't understand genius. And here I am, saying, "Please put him in this hospital." Because we didn't know what to do.'

The Devil and Daniel Johnston is a tribute not only to Johnston and his music, but to his friends and especially his parents, Mabel and Bill, who have

spent a lifetime doing their best in the midst of un-
bearable stress.

Then there was Don Van Vliet, Captain Beefheart,
who ruled over his band with a tyrannical fury. For
his album *Trout Mask Replica* he rented a house in
Woodland Hills, Los Angeles, and forced his musicians to eat only a cup of soya beans a day. For eight
months they weren't allowed to leave the house at
all, except for once a week when one of them was
permitted to briefly go and get groceries. He would
psychologically break his drummer and bass player
down by yelling repeatedly in their faces, 'You hate
your mother!' for thirty-hour stretches.

Peter, Lenny and I rented a disused railway station
for a while just outside the Alton Towers theme park,
near Stoke, so we could write. It was there Peter told
me a haunting story about a band called The Shaggs.
It was a story he only half-remembered from something he'd read years before, but it was so strange
I felt compelled to fly to The Shaggs' home town,
Fremont, New Hampshire, to try and meet them.

•

Nowadays Dot Wiggin is a cleaner in her local church. You wouldn't know from meeting her or her sister Betty that they once recorded about the strangest record ever made.

Fremont looked as gentle and as unassuming as they did. The main display in the Historical Museum commemorated how Fremont was the first place in the world where a B52 bomber had crashed but nobody was killed. 'B52 bombers had crashed elsewhere,' Matthew Thomas, the town historian, told me when I'd visited the museum the night before, 'but people had died. In Fremont, nobody died. That's what made Fremont pretty unique with that episode.'

I took a walk with Dot and Betty to their house. Or the place where it used to be before the new owners burnt it to the ground so they could build a new house further up the land. The grass had never grown back so you could still see the outline – the ghost of a house. It was there they told me their story.

When Dot and Betty were children there was no music in their lives. No music and no friends outside

Betty Wiggin, Jon Ronson, Dot Wiggin

the family. Their father Austin wouldn't allow it. 'We couldn't go to dances or anything,' Dot told me. 'We just stayed home. He didn't want us to have a social life. He was afraid we'd get too involved on the outside.'

'Which we would have,' Betty said.

Given his devout bearing, the announcement he made over dinner one night sometime during the mid-1960s came very much out of the blue. He told his daughters that he'd just returned from his mother's house where she'd read his palm and divined from it that the sisters were going to be in one of the most successful girl groups in America. He was therefore taking them out of school so they could practise. Relentlessly. From morning until night. Until they were ready.

'We practised during the day when he worked,' Dot told me, 'and then when he came home from work we practised. We practised until he liked it. If he didn't like it we practised over and over. Usually on Saturdays too.'

'Did he ever ask you if you wanted to do it?' I asked.

'No!' Dot and Betty laughed.

'Did you sometimes think your father was nuts?'
I asked.

There was a short silence. 'Yeah, that would fit it,'
Betty said.

'Obsessive,' said Dot. 'Very obsessive with the
music.' And with exercises too: 'Jumping-jacks,' said
Dot. 'Push-ups. We had to stay in shape in case we
ever got to be on *The Ed Sullivan Show*.'

'When you think back on those rehearsals, what
comes into your mind?' I asked.

'That I didn't want to do it,' said Betty.

It lasted five years. And then, just as suddenly
as Austin had announced the strategy, he one day
declared them ready.

'We didn't think we were ready,' Dot told me.

Still, they drove to the recording studio – a girl
group of Kaspar Hausers, out in the countryside,
home-schooled, separated from society, pretty much
inventing music from scratch. If you've heard practically no music and then you're told to create music,
what would it sound like?

*

It sounded, as Bonnie Raitt said of them decades later, like music performed by 'castaways on their own musical desert island'. The singer in the band NRBQ, Terry Adams, later described them to me as having 'a different rhythmic approach, which acknowledges what's going on but ignores it at the same time. There are no harmonies. It's always unison singing. Two voices and one guitar playing exactly the same melody at all times.'

'Is that unusual?' I asked him.

'Very,' he said.

Their music is of course available online. I suggest the song 'Philosophy of the World' as a starting point. It sounds like space aliens pretending to be human. It sounds, too, I now realized, like the music of abuse. And the cruelty only spread once the album came out and Austin forced his daughters to be the house band at the local dances.

'We'd have soda cans shot at us on stage,' Dot said, 'kids telling us how bad we were, how our music was trash, how it hurt their ears, how we didn't know what we were doing . . .'

But the music wasn't trash – it was something altogether different. They were doing it against their will, they weren't very good, they massively over-rehearsed, they had no musical influences – it was like a child throwing a bunch of chemicals randomly onto a Bunsen burner and the strangest bubbles ensuing.

In 1975 Austin dropped dead of a heart attack at the age of forty-seven. The instant the sisters heard the news they disbanded The Shaggs, determined never to play again.

And they never would have – their music would have been lost for ever – except that Terry Adams somehow came across a copy of *Philosophy of the World* some twenty years later, was mesmerized by what he heard, and decided to drive to Fremont to try and convince them to let him re-release it.

'My brother and my drummer and I got in the car and took a six-hour drive, just blindly,' Terry Adams told me when I later contacted him. 'We went to the library and asked around until we could find them.'

Eventually Dot and her then husband Fred agreed to a rendezvous at a local Pizza Hut. Terry and his brother and the band's drummer sat on one side of the table, with Dot and Fred on the other. Terry nervously gave them his pitch. Dot and Fred listened. And finally, when he was done, Fred leaned forward, businessman to businessman, and said, 'Well how much is this going to cost us?'

There was a silence. 'No,' Terry explained. '*We're* going to pay *you*.'

Betty didn't want anything to do with it. It was all just too painful. But then, when Terry Adams released the album and the reviews came in, even she began to doubt her own inabilities. Kurt Cobain, in his list of fifty favourite albums of all time, put *Philosophy of the World* at number five (just below the Pixies and Iggy and the Stooges and above the Sex Pistols and R.E.M.).

Jonathan Richman said one Shaggs song was 'worth ten "professional" songs. The Shaggs convince me that they're the real thing when they sing.'

The jazz composer Carla Bley said, 'They bring my mind to a complete halt.' Nothing much happened after that. The album sold pretty well. They performed one or two shows. Susan Orlean wrote about them for the *New Yorker*. A stage musical – *Philosophy of the World* – was written and performed in New York and Los Angeles. Their film rights were bought, although no film has yet been made. I turned my meeting with them into a documentary for BBC Radio Four. But, basically, it was a just flurry and everything went back to normal for Dot and Betty.

'When did you first listen to *Philosophy of the World* and think, "This is actually quite good"?' I asked Betty towards the end of my day with them.

She looked at me and hesitated. 'I still don't think it's good,' she said.

No trace of The Shaggs' story made it to our Frank film, but something did: for all our mythologizing, the margins can be painful and some people are there because they have no choice.

•

A week after I returned from Fremont, I saw Frank Sidebottom's name trending on Twitter. I'd spent a couple of years living with the words Frank Sidebottom every day, so this didn't seem at all odd. It was just his name on a screen like every day. I clicked on the link and it said 'Frank Sidebottom dead'. I wondered why Chris had decided to kill off Frank and why Twitter cared enough to make it a trending topic. So I clicked on another link:

Stars lead tributes as Frank Sidebottom comic dies at 54

Chris Sievey, famous as his alter ego Frank Sidebottom, was found collapsed at his home in Hale early yesterday. It is understood that his girlfriend called an ambulance and he was taken to Wythenshawe Hospital, where his death was confirmed.

Manchester Evening News, 22 June 2010

When I'd told Chris at our last meeting in Kentish Town how thin he looked and he shrugged and said it was a mystery and he seemed pleased – he didn't know it then, but it had been throat cancer.

Frank Sidebottom comic faces pauper's funeral

The comic genius behind Mancunian legend Frank Sidebottom is facing a pauper's funeral after dying virtually penniless. Chris Sievey had no assets and little money in the bank, his family have revealed.

Manchester Evening News, 23 June 2010

A pauper's funeral? What did that involve? A journey back in time two hundred years? Later, Chris's son Sterling told me that the hospital bereavement officer had described a pauper's funeral to him as 'not as bad as it sounded. There'd be a coffin but it wouldn't be coffin shaped. It would be more like a rectangular box. Like a cargo crate or something.'

'What about a service?' I asked Sterling.

'No,' he said. 'No real service. And there wouldn't have been a gravestone.'

I sent out a single tweet, saying that for a few thousand pounds Chris could be spared a pauper's funeral. Within an hour 554 people had donated £6,950.03. An hour later it was 1,108 donors and £14,018.90. By the end of the day it was 1,632 donors raising a total of £21,631.55. One blogger wrote of the donors: 'I found the speed of events breathtaking, and genuinely inspiring that so many people could reach into their pockets in tribute to a man who many won't have met, spoken to, or even seen his face. It's nice to know there are so many kind-hearted people out there & wonderful to see another example of how social networks can be used in a positive, inspirational way.'

The money we raised that day was more than enough to bury and exhume and rebury Chris half a dozen times. The donations never stopped. We had to stop them. People still wanted to give but there was nothing to give for.

A Timperley village councillor, Neil Taylor, started his own campaign to raise money for a memorial statue – Frank cast in bronze. He sent me photographs of its journey from the foundry in the Czech Republic to its final resting place outside Johnson's the dry cleaners in Timperley. In the photographs Frank looked like he'd been disturbingly kidnapped but was fine with it.

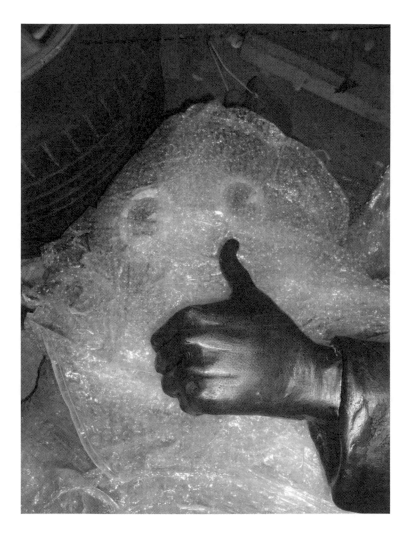

Frank statue

The unveiling

In eight weeks' time our Frank film, starring Michael Fassbender, Maggie Gyllenhaal and Domhnall Gleeson, will be premiered at the Sundance Film Festival. As I prepare to go to it I remember something Chris once said to me. It was late one night, and we were in the van, reminiscing about a show we'd played a few weeks earlier at JB's nightclub in Dudley, West Midlands. It was very poorly attended. There can't have been more than fifteen people in the audience. One of them produced a ball, the audience split into teams and, ignoring us, played a game. In the van Chris smiled wistfully.

'That Dudley gig,' he said.

'Ah ha?' I said.

'Best show we ever played,' he said.

THE END

Frank, the movie